Getting Ahead by Staying Behind: 175 Ways to Live Beneath your Means

I0416041

Eric Santaiti

ISBN: 1492387762
ISBN-13: 978-1492387763

Introduction

Do you want to improve your financial position over the course of a significant time-horizon?

Maybe this book can help. The author has lived almost his entire life in an area of the USA where there is a high cost of living. His parents and grandparents were never wealthy, but he learned from them early on about the basics of saving money, most importantly discipline. As he grew older, he accelerated his learning in personal finance on his own and eventually managed to sextuple his own net worth - with zero debt outside of a mortgage - in a ten year span.

To him, it was actually fun watching his financials grow. After a while, he decided to share his learnings and ideas so that others could experience similar results. Mind you, the advice here is not about ceasing spending altogether; it is about thinking through your spending, adjusting daily habits, and making wise decisions that add up in savings over time.

So, consider the following advice in your situation; if you can apply many of them in a disciplined manner, over time you will reap the benefits. Good luck and happy saving!

Table of Contents

I. Your Health

- ☐ Activity & Inactivity

- ☐ Consumption

- ☐ Health Plan

Your Health: Activity & Inactivity

- ☐ **Exercise regularly.** Exercise increases your wellness and longevity, in turn helping prevent injury and health complications as we age, thus saving money.

- ☐ **Invest in a comfortable bed and pillows.** Better sleep means better recovery from daily stresses.

- ☐ **Invest in your own exercise equipment.** Assuming you have the space, owning equipment in the home can be much cheaper than a gym membership.

- ☐ **Obtain at least 8 hours of sleep every night.** Adequate sleep time enables your brain to process your life experiences and your body to recover.

- ☐ **Stretch / warm up appropriately around exercise.** This is critical in order to prevent injury.

- ☐ **Walk every day in the sunshine.** The fresh air and natural Vitamin D is free and good for the body and your mood.

- **Buy what you need and eat what you buy.** Throwing away food – spoiled or not – is costly.

- **Don't abuse drugs.** They are expensive and can have negative effects on your body.

- **Don't abuse alcohol.** It is expensive and can have negative effects on your body.

- **Don't drink too much coffee.** It is expensive and can have negative effects on your body.

- **Don't smoke.** It is expensive and can have negative effects on your body.

- **Drink more water instead of soft drinks.** It is usually cheaper and more healthful than carbonated beverages.

- **Eat more healthful foods in general.** Eat sensible portions of healthy foods so that you spend more time living and not in hospitals.

- ☐ **Ask your dentist for free oral supplies.** It is likely he/she is willing to supply you with a toothbrush, toothpaste, or floss at no cost.

- ☐ **Ask your doctor for a few free samples.** Sometimes he/she can offer a drug on a trial basis at no cost.

- ☐ **Check out local inexpensive clinics.** Occasionally they offer discounted services compared to your doctor's office.

- ☐ **Pick an appropriate health plan.** Then use only those institutions/health professionals that are in the network.

- ☐ **Try to keep the same doctor as you age.** He/she would possess your full health picture for better diagnoses.

- ☐ **Utilize your employer's health care plan.** They can purchase health coverage at a lower cost than you can alone.

- ☐ **Utilize your employer's health spending program.** Used carefully, they can save you much money over the long-term.

Notes

II. Your Shopping

☐ Eating In and Out

☐ At the Stores

☐ **Bring a reusable cup or mug to the casual eatery.** You might be able to fill it up with water for free or at a discount.

☐ **Cook larger meals.** Then you have cheap leftovers from the freezer and you use your appliances less.

☐ **Do not order dessert every time in the restaurant.** They are usually very pricey.

☐ **Eat slightly smaller portions.** You will save money on food – and not end up throwing any away.

☐ **Re-use gently used napkins.** Turn them over for re-use, or try cloth napkins.

☐ **Take home any unused napkins when you eat out.** Then use them at home.

☐ **Before buying a discretionary item, pause.** If practical, wait at least a week to keep money longer.

☐ **Buy generic-brand products when possible.** If they are of acceptable quality, they can be much cheaper.

☐ **Buy in larger quantities / sizes of a product.** The per unit cost is generally cheaper.

☐ **Buy large single purchases only when on sale.** Or only when you find a discount.

☐ **Buy college/reference books that are used.** Pre-owned books are considerably cheaper than new ones.

☐ **Check out reviews online for a product/service.** Researching online prior to purchasing can minimize bad deals.

☐ **Compare prices based on unit price.** This allows you to compare prices on an even level.

☐ **Compare prices online.** When this is possible, you can find quickly the lowest price available.

☐ **Don't buy anything on impulse.** Sometimes we realize we don't really need it or find a better value later.

☐ **If buying online, take advantage of rebates.** There are free online rebate programs available.

☐ **Join the savings club at your favorite stores.** They usually offer free discounts and special sales.

☐ **Save your paper shopping bags.** Return them to the store for a rebate, if available.

☐ **Search online for coupon or promo codes.** It is a quick and easy way to save money prior to completing an online purchase.

☐ **Seek out consumer benefit programs.** For example, free movie tickets might be offered from your cable provider.

☐ **Seek out free web-based software.** They might suit your needs without purchasing anything over the counter.

☐ **Try finding media at the local library.** They can offer books and movies at a reduced or no cost.

☐ **Try checking out yard sales or thrift stores.** Bargains can be found.

☐ **Use a good electric razor.** Disposable blades cost much more.

☐ **Use coupons.** Supermarkets print them on flyers and websites can offer a printable coupon as well.

☐ **Use free product samples.** They can be found in the mail or in the stores.

☐ **Utilize cloth/canvas shopping bags.** Some grocery stores offer a small discount, or you avoid charges for bags at the store.

☐ **Wait some time for prices to come down.** This is especially relevant for new electronic devices.

☐ **You can make your own cards.** Greeting/holiday cards (even envelopes) can be made with scrap paper and you can put a personal touch on them.

Notes

III. The Five-Discount Purchase

Usually I feel too smart to pay full price for anything. So occasionally I find a way to achieve five discounts on a single (online) purchase. How? Here are the steps:

1. Know what you really need, and how much.

2. Find an online store that currently offers a sale on the item. *Discount #1*

3. Purchase only if you have enough in that online shopping cart that allows for free shipping. *Discount #2*

4. Search online for a coupon code or promotional code, and apply it. *Discount #3*

5. Execute the purchase via an online rebate site. *Discount #4*

6. Finally purchase with a credit card that offers a rebate on everything you buy. *Discount #5*

Over time, savings add up!

IV. Your Money

- ☐ Clothes

- ☐ Your Employer

- ☐ Rates and Cards

- ☐ Taxes

- ☐ General

- ☐ **Accept hand-me-down garments.** Use them when you can because they are free.

- ☐ **Buy clothes when they are out of season.** That is when they are discounted.

- ☐ **Mix and match existing clothing items.** Try creating new outfit combinations prior to purchasing more.

- ☐ **Re-use your worn-out jeans or sweats as shorts.** They are perfect for dirty jobs around the house.

- ☐ **Save your child's stuff for another child.** Clothes and even clean baby toys are good examples.

- ☐ **Take good care of your clothes.** They will last longer.

- ☐ **Try selling at a consignment shop.** Those shops might be suitable for your gently-used rare apparel such as dresses.

- ☐ **Use your old worn-out cotton clothes as rags.** Use your old whites for cleaning jobs in the house or garage prior to tossing them away.

- **Bring your own lunch to the workplace.** Leftovers or peanut-butter & jelly sandwiches are economical.

- **Check for employer discount programs.** Large companies can negotiate discounts on things such as vehicles or theater tickets.

- **If you need it, buy your employer's product.** Companies sometimes offer to employees their own product for sale at a huge discount.

- **Piggy-back on expense-paid business trips.** If allowed, add personal excursions to business travel.

- **Set up a direct deposit of your paycheck.** Have it conveniently deposited into your checking or highest-interest account.

- **Try negotiating a better pay rate.** Use solid research to back it up; the worst result is a "No".

- **Utilize your company's retirement plan.** Assuming it is available to you, consider it "free" money.

- **Watch for leftover supplies at your employer.** They might be willing to give away something you need.

☐ **Don't carry more credit cards than you need.** Holding too many cards can hurt your credit score.

☐ **Make saving automatic.** Set up automatic transfers from a lower to a higher interest account.

☐ **Pay off highest-interest debt loans first.** Do check the numbers first with a financial professional to confirm your strategy.

☐ **Pay your bills on time, every time.** This will ensure good credit history.

☐ **Save your money and buy when you can afford it.** The unfavorable alternative is financing a big purchase with a loan plus interest.

☐ **Shop around for the best interest rates.** Do this for all of your banking and investment accounts.

☐ **Utilize a credit card that offers rebates.** Also avoid cards that charge an annual fee.

- **If you have young kids, save for college early.** Check out government-sponsored savings plans.

- **Take advantage of tax rules.** Specifically, leverage tax savings in your retirement accounts.

- **Track your business expenses.** Be sure to get reimbursed for them as soon as possible.

- **Track your charitable donations.** They can potentially be written off against income at tax-time.

- **Track your eligible home improvements.** Usually you can write them off against home capital gains when you sell.

- **Track your unreimbursed health expenses.** Itemize them on your taxes for a possible reduction.

- **Try free tax preparation software.** Also seek out free tax centers (e.g. for seniors) prior to hiring an accountant.

- **After a purchase, voice your legitimate complaint.** The company might offer a discount on future purchases as compensation.

- **Before hiring a financial advisor, find free tools.** Online resources and tools for managing your money are abundant.

- **Deposit your cash/checks as soon as possible.** That way, they can generate interest as soon as possible.

- **Diversify your investment accounts.** Be aggressive at first, and then be more conservative as you near retirement or cash-out time.

- **Buy "forever" stamps from the Postal Service.** They protect you against price increases.

- **If all else fails, try negotiating!** The worst result is a "No".

☐ **Pay your bills online as much as possible.** You will use less checks, envelopes, and stamps.

☐ **Read the fine print on contracts.** Always do this before you sign an agreement in order to minimize getting ripped-off.

☐ **Research the feasibility of selling online.** Prior to throwing something away, maybe you can sell to someone who values it more.

☐ **Re-use gift wrapping paper, bows, boxes, etc.** Use them for a subsequent occasion or the following season.

☐ **Save and invest your money as early as possible.** Leverage time to grow your money.

☐ **Seek out free local recreation programs.** They might be just as good as costlier, larger multi-town leagues.

☐ **Join frequent buyer programs.** They cost nothing to enroll and will pay off eventually.

☐ **Get a job and go to work, every day.** But don't forget to take time off!

☐ **Stay with friends or family on special trips.** If possible, this saves money and offers an opportunity to re-connect with loved ones.

☐ **Take a vacation primarily when it is discounted.** Often, you can save money by bundling reservations through a single agency.

☐ **Track your finances.** You can only manage something if you measure it; track your financial status and celebrate achievements.

☐ **Try chewing half the stick of gum at a time.** This will stretch the life of the pack.

Notes

V. Your Residence

- ☐ Water

- ☐ Appliances

- ☐ Other Utilities

- ☐ General

Your Residence: Water

☐ **Change your shower head to a low-flow one.** You will save on your water bill.

☐ **Fill your clothes washer and dishwasher fully.** Do this whenever possible to minimize water use and energy usage.

☐ **Set up a system to collect rainwater or graywater.** If feasible, the water could be re-used for toilets and garden irrigation.

☐ **Shut off water when not in use.** For example, do not let it run while brushing your teeth.

☐ **Take shorter showers.** This is an easy way to reduce water consumption.

☐ **Tighten leaky faucets.** Drips of water slowly add up, and they can be an easy fix.

☐ **Use cold water when washing.** Using cold water to wash hands, clothes, etc. as much as possible can save on your heating bill.

☐ **Dry your clothes outdoors whenever possible.** The dryer is one of the most expensive appliances to run.

☐ **If affordable, replace your old appliances.** Newer, more efficient ones can offer long-term savings.

☐ **Maintain your appliances well (e.g. lubrication).** They will operate more efficiently and longer.

☐ **Make sure your A/C and dryer filters are clean.** Clean them regularly for efficient operation and to avoid a hazardous situation.

☐ **Put your appliances on power switches.** Switching off major appliances (TV, computer, etc.) when not in use and overnight prevents power leakage.

☐ **Run your washer/dryer at smart times.** In the summer months, it is best in the early morning or evening.

☐ **See to it that the A/C compressor sits in the shade.** In the summer months, outdoor units will operate more efficiently when the sun is blocked.

☐ **Use fans instead of air conditioning units.** Do this as much as possible, or use them together.

☐ **Cancel your landline if possible.** This is ideal if you can use your mobile phone exclusively.

☐ **Check for sensible phone plans.** Enroll in plans that make sense financially based on how you use your phone.

☐ **Install storm doors at entrances.** They can prevent heat loss.

☐ **Install solar panels, if feasible.** They will offer you long-term energy efficiency and potential profitability.

☐ **Insulate carefully your windows / walls / pipes.** Proper insulation will reduce your heating and cooling bills.

☐ **Open/shut your shades at appropriate times.** This is another way to help reduce your heating and cooling bills.

☐ **Plant trees in smart places around the house.** They increase shade on hot days.

☐ **Reduce the upper temperature of the water heater.** You likely do not need running water to reach boiling-hot temperatures.

☐ **Request an energy audit.** Your electric utility might offer it at no cost to customers.

☐ **Set your thermostats modestly.** You will save on heating and cooling costs.

☐ **Shut off your electronics overnight.** If you turn off your mobile phone, for example, it will use less energy and need to be charged less.

- □ **Try the "time of day" rate program.** Some electric companies offer it and it could make sense depending on your usage habits.

- □ **Turn off your lights.** Do this when you leave the room and especially overnight or when traveling.

- □ **Use efficient lighting.** For example, install CFL or LED bulbs over incandescent ones at home to save energy costs.

- □ **Upgrade your windows.** They will improve climate control, not to mention noise-dampening.

- □ **Wear slippers and layers of clothing.** In the winter, you will be able to lower your thermostat; in the summer, wear less/light clothes to keep cool.

☐ **Accept hand-me-down furniture.** Clean them up and put them to use, if you can.

☐ **Avoid using shampoo & conditioner every day.** You can save on those products.

☐ **Before hiring a contractor, seek out videos.** Many "how to" videos are posted online for help on minor household projects.

☐ **Buy a smaller home.** It is cheaper to maintain and your utility bills will be lower.

☐ **Compost your organic waste.** You will have free fertilizer for your garden if you have one.

☐ **Don't put the garbage out every day.** You can save on garbage bags if you do not have to do this.

☐ **Find a new use for household objects.** Jars or trays or boxes, for example, can be used for storage or creative projects.

☐ **Live in a less expensive area.** You can lower your cost of living in an area in less demand, for example.

☐ **Lower your thermostat prior to hosting a party.** People generate a lot of heat too.

☐ **Make mobile phone calls during off-peak hours.** They generally don't count toward your minutes.

☐ **Own a hair-cutter set.** Have a friend cut your hair at home, or cut your own.

☐ **Postpone non-urgent/non-essential home repairs.** The act of postponing upgrades and the like allows you to hold onto money longer.

☐ **Recycle for cash.** Some states still offer a refund.

☐ **Recycle properly.** Recycling helps reduce waste disposal costs and thus could mean lower local taxes and retail prices.

☐ **Save your shopping/produce bags.** You can re-use them as waste bags in the house, for example, bread bags for pet waste.

☐ **Set up an automatic withdrawal for bills.** Do it for your mortgage payment, for example, so no checks or mailings are used.

☐ **Shop around for homeowner's insurance.** Make sure that your coverage matches your need.

☐ **Split the paper towel in half.** Halve the paper towel before cleaning and you will use less in the long run.

☐ **Squeeze out every bit of product from the bottle.** Don't leave any product to waste.

☐ **Submit a real estate tax appeal.** This can pay off if you are in a good position to do so.

☐ **Take home those bathroom products from hotels.** Use those small bottles or soap for personal use or for guests (but don't steal!).

☐ **Try to live in an area with cleaner air and water.** Better air and water quality helps increase general wellness and minimize environmental health risk.

Notes

VI. Your Vehicle

☐ Driving & Fuel

☐ General

☐ **Avoid driving engines above efficient speeds.** Fifty-five miles per hour is the optimal speed for many vehicles.

☐ **Bike or walk if possible.** Don't use the vehicle if you are merely visiting your neighbor or the community recreation center down the block.

☐ **Buy a more fuel-efficient vehicle.** You could save thousands in fuel costs over the life of the vehicle.

☐ **Carpool when possible.** This is especially smart on long trips.

☐ **Compare the cost of public modes versus driving.** Sometimes public transportation is cheaper.

☐ **Drive less often.** Go out only when it is necessary, and plan your trips smartly so that you can make multiple stops over the shortest total distance.

☐ **Drive slower.** By accelerating and decelerating gradually, you use less fuel and extend parts life.

☐ **Empty your vehicle as much as possible.** More weight means lower fuel economy.

□ **Find a fuel station that offers lower prices.** And avoid stations that offer poor-quality fuel.

□ **Move.** If you are able to move closer to work to reduce your commute or to move away from high traffic areas, then your fuel usage will be lower.

□ **Obey the traffic laws and speed limits.** Thus avoid tickets and fines.

□ **Reduce drag.** Swallowing up air slows you down, so close your windows at high speeds.

□ **Release the accelerator downhill.** Allow gravity and momentum to propel you forward whenever possible.

□ **Seek out special commuter plans.** Sometimes there are plans available for discounted tolls or train tickets.

□ **Shut off the engine while idling.** If safe to do so, turn off the vehicle while waiting in a line.

□ **Utilize cruise control.** It is great on long trips and open roads and helps reduce fuel consumption.

□ **Work from home occasionally.** If this is allowable, you can eliminate commuting costs.

☐ **Attend a driver's safety class.** Most insurance companies offer a discount as long as you can show proof of attendance.

☐ **Bundle your vehicle and home insurance.** If you combine them under one insurer, you can save money on both.

☐ **Buy reliable vehicles.** You can save money on maintenance costs long-term.

☐ **Buy vehicles with safety features.** Features such as an alarm or air bags typically translate into insurance discounts and can minimize serious injury in a crash.

☐ **Maintain your vehicle.** Peform regular maintenance on your vehicle such as diagnostics and tire pressure check-ups to prolong its life.

☐ **Purchase a vehicle slightly used instead of new.** You can save thousands on a vehicle up-front.

☐ **Shop around for vehicle insurance.** Also consider a high deductible, which lowers your premium.

Notes

www.ingramcontent.com/pod-product-compliance
Lightning Source LLC
Chambersburg PA
CBHW071004290526
45795CB00005B/1767